Wherever her fighting lines are thrust or spread!
They call us proud? Look at our English Rose!
Shedders of blood? Where hath our own been spared?
Shopkeepers? Our accompt the high GOD knows.
Close? In our bounty half the world hath shared.
They hate us, and they envy? Envy and hate
Should drive them to the PIT'S edge? Be it so!
That race is damned which misesteems its fate;
And this, in GOD'S good time, they all shall know,
And know you too, you good green ENGLAND, then
Mother of mothering girls and governing men!

INVICTUS

Out of the night that covers me,
Black as the pit from pole to pole,
I thank whatever gods may be
For my unconquerable soul.

In the fell clutch of circumstance
I have not winced nor cried aloud.
Under the bludgeonings of chance
My head is bloody, but unbowed.

Beyond this place of wrath and tears
Looms but the Horror of the shade,
And yet the menace of the years
Finds and shall find me unafraid.

It matters not how strait the gate,
How charged with punishments the scroll,
I am the master of my fate,
I am the captain of my soul.

HAWTHORN AND LAVENDER

ENVOY

My songs were once of the sunrise:
They shouted it over the bar;
First-footing the dawns, they flourished,
And flamed with the morning star.

My songs are now of the sunset:
Their brows are touched with light,
But their feet are lost in the shadows
And wet with the dews of night.

Yet for the joy in their making
Take them, O fond and true,
And for his sake who made them

Let them be dear to You.

Largo Espressivo
In sumptuous chords, and strange,
Through rich yet poignant harmonies:
Subtle and strong browns, reds
Magnificent with death and the pride of death,
Thin, clamant greens
And delicate yellows that exhaust
The exquisite chromatics of decay:
From ruining gardens, from reluctant woods
Dear, multitudinously reluctant woods!
And sering margents, forced
To be lean and bare and perished grace by grace,
And flower by flower discharmed,
Comes, to a purpose none,
Not even the Scorner, which is the Fool, can blink,
The dead-march of the year.

Dead things and dying! Now the long-laboured soul
Listens, and pines. But never a note of hope
Sounds: whether in those high,
Transcending unisons of resignation
That speed the sovran sun,
As he goes southing, weakening, minishing,
Almighty in obedience; or in those
Small, sorrowful colloquies
Of bronze and russet and gold,
Colour with colour, dying things with dead,
That break along this visual orchestra:
As in that other one, the audible,
Horn answers horn, hautboy and violin
Talk, and the 'cello calls the clarionet
And flute, and the poor heart is glad.
There is no hope in these only despair.

Then, destiny in act, ensues
That most tremendous passage in the score:
When hangman rains and winds have wrought
Their worst, and, the brave lights gone down,
The low strings, the brute brass, the sullen drums
Sob, grovel, and curse themselves
Silent. . . .
But on the spirit of Man
And on the heart of the World there falls
A strange, half-desperate peace:
A war-worn, militant, gray jubilance

The Poetry Of William Ernest Henley - Volume 2

William Ernest Henley was born in Gloucester on 23 August 1849, the eldest of six children.

Between 1861 and 1867, Henley was a pupil at the Crypt Grammar School. It was also from this time that William suffered from tuberculosis of the bone that resulted in the amputation of his left leg below the knee in 1868–69.

Frequent illness often kept him from school, although the misfortunes of his father's business also contributed. In 1867, Henley passed the Oxford Local Schools Examination and moved to London to establish himself as a journalist. However, this quest was interrupted over the next eight years by long stays in the hospital as the disease spread to his right foot. The opinion was that a second amputation would save his life. William sought a second opinion from the pioneering surgeon Joseph Lister. After three years in the hospital (1873–75), during which Henley wrote and published the poems collected as In Hospital, he was discharged. Although the treatment was not a complete cure, Henley enjoyed a relatively active life for almost thirty more years.

In 1875 William wrote his classic poem "Invictus" which is evidently based on his illness and was only published in 1888 in his first volume of poems, Book of Verses,

On 22 January 1878, he married Hannah (Anna) Johnson Boyle. Their sickly young daughter, Margaret, was immortalized by J. M. Barrie in his children's classic, Peter Pan. Unable to speak clearly, young Margaret had called her friend Barrie her "fwendy-wendy", resulting in the use of "Wendy" in the book. Margaret died at age 5 and buried at the country estate of her father's friend, Harry Cockayne Cust, in Cockayne Hatley, Bedfordshire.

William was now to earn his living as a publisher. In 1889 he became editor of the Scots Observer, and precursor of the National Observer (UK). After its headquarters were transferred to London in 1891, it became the National Observer and remained under Henley's editorship until 1893. The paper had almost as many writers as readers, said Henley, and its fame was confined mainly to the literary class, but it was a lively and influential contributor to the literary life of its era.

As a poet and playwright Henley wrote a great deal. Mainly admired for 'Invictus' there are many other poems and plays in his works which are just as good.

William Ernest Henley died of tuberculosis in 1903 at the age of 53 at his home in Woking, and his ashes were interred in his daughter's grave in the churchyard at Cockayne Hatley in Bedfordshire.

Index Of Poems

DEDICATION

Ask me not how they came,
These songs of love and death,
These dreams of a futile stage,
These thumb-nails seen in the street:
Ask me not how nor why,
But take them for your own,
Dear Wife of twenty years,
Knowing, O, who so well?
You it was made the man
That made these songs of love,
Death, and the trivial rest:
So that, your love elsewhere,
These songs, or bad or good
How should they ever have been?

WORTHING, July 31, 1901.

PROLOGUE

These to the glory and praise of the green land
That bred my women, and that holds my dead,
ENGLAND, and with her the strong broods that stand

In the unkind, implacable tyranny
Of Winter, the obscene,
Old, crapulous Regent, who in his loins
O, who but feels he carries in his loins
The wild, sweet-blooded, wonderful harlot, Spring?

I.
Low low
Over a perishing after-glow,
A thin, red shred of moon
Trailed. In the windless air
The poplars all ranked lean and chill.
The smell of winter loitered there,
And the Year's heart felt still.
Yet not so far away
Seemed the mad Spring,
But that, as lovers will,
I let my laughing heart go play,
As it had been a fond maid's frolicking;
And, turning thrice the gold I'd got,
In the good gloom
Solemnly wished me what?
What, and with whom?

II
Moon of half-candied meres
And flurrying, fading snows;
Moon of unkindly rains,
Wild skies, and troubled vanes;
When the Norther snarls and bites,
And the lone moon walks a-cold,
And the lawns grizzle o' nights,
And wet fogs search the fold:
Here in this heart of mine
A dream that warms like wine,
A dream one other knows,
Moon of the roaring weirs
And the sip-sopping close,
February Fill-Dyke,
Shapes like a royal rose
A red, red rose!

O, but the distance clears!
O, but the daylight grows!
Soon shall the pied wind-flowers
Babble of greening hours,
Primrose and daffodil
Yearn to a fathering sun,
The lark have all his will,
The thrush be never done,
And April, May, and June

Go to the same blythe tune
As this blythe dream of mine!
Moon when the crocus peers,
Moon when the violet blows,
February Fair-Maid,
Haste, and let come the rose
Let come the rose!

III
The night dislimns, and breaks
Like snows slow thawn;
An evil wind awakes
On lea and lawn;
The low East quakes; and hark!
Out of the kindless dark,
A fierce, protesting lark,
High in the horror of dawn!

A shivering streak of light,
A scurry of rain:
Bleak day from bleaker night
Creeps pinched and fain;
The old gloom thins and dies,
And in the wretched skies
A new gloom, sick to rise,
Sprawls, like a thing in pain.

And yet, what matter say!
The shuddering trees,
The Easter-stricken day,
The sodden leas?
The good bird, wing and wing
With Time, finds heart to sing,
As he were hastening
The swallow o'er the seas.

IV
It came with the year's first crocus
In a world of winds and snows
Because it would, because it must,
Because of life and time and lust;
And a year's first crocus served my turn
As well as the year's first rose.

The March rack hurries and hectors,
The March dust heaps and blows;
But the primrose flouts the daffodil,
And here's the patient violet still;
And the year's first crocus brought me luck,
So hey for the year's first rose!

V

The good South-West on sea-worn wings
Comes shepherding the good rain;
The brave Sea breaks, and glooms, and swings,
A weltering, glittering plain.

Sound, Sea of England, sound and shine,
Blow, English Wind, amain,
Till in this old, gray heart of mine
The Spring need wake again!

VI

In the red April dawn,
In the wild April weather,
From brake and thicket and lawn
The birds sing all together.

The look of the hoyden Spring
Is pinched and shrewish and cold;
But all together they sing
Of a world that can never be old:

Of a world still young still young!
Whose last word won't be said,
Nor her last song dreamed and sung,
Till her last true lover's dead!

VII

The April sky sags low and drear,
The April winds blow cold,
The April rains fall gray and sheer,
And yeanlings keep the fold.

But the rook has built, and the song-birds quire,
And over the faded lea
The lark soars glorying, gyre on gyre,
And he is the bird for me!

For he sings as if from his watchman's height
He saw, this blighting day,
The far vales break into colour and light
From the banners and arms of May.

VIII

Shadow and gleam on the Downland
Under the low Spring sky,
Shadow and gleam in my spirit
Why?

A bird, in his nest rejoicing,
Cheers and flatters and woos:

A fresh voice flutters my fancy
Whose?

And the humour of April frolics
And bickers in blade and bough
O, to meet for the primal kindness
Now!

IX
The wind on the wold,
With sea-scents and sea-dreams attended,
Is wine!
The air is as gold
In elixir it takes so the splendid
Sunshine!

O, the larks in the blue!
How the song of them glitters, and glances,
And gleams!
The old music sounds new
And it's O, the wild Spring, and his chances
And dreams!

There's a lift in the blood
O, this gracious, and thirsting, and aching
Unrest!
All life's at the bud,
And my heart, full of April, is breaking
My breast.

X
Deep in my gathering garden
A gallant thrush has built;
And his quaverings on the stillness
Like light made song are spilt.

They gleam, they glint, they sparkle,
They glitter along the air,
Like the song of a sunbeam netted
In a tangle of red-gold hair.

And I long, as I laugh and listen,
For the angel-hour that shall bring
My part, pre-ordained and appointed,
In the miracle of Spring.

XI
What doth the blackbird in the boughs
Sing all day to his nested spouse?
What but the song of his old Mother-Earth,
In her mighty humour of lust and mirth?

'Love and God's will go wing and wing,
And as for death, is there any such thing?'
In the shadow of death,
So, at the beck of the wizard Spring
The dear bird saith
So the bird saith!

Caught with us all in the nets of fate,
So the sweet wretch sings early and late;
And, O my fairest, after all,
The heart of the World's in his innocent call.
The will of the World's with him wing and wing:
'Life – life - life! 'Tis the sole great thing
This side of death,
Heart on heart in the wonder of Spring!'
So the bird saith
The wise bird saith!

XII
This world, all hoary
With song and story,
Rolls in a glory
Of youth and mirth;
Above and under
Clothed on with wonder.
Sunrise and thunder,
And death and birth.
His broods befriending
With grace unending
And gifts transcending
A god's at play,
Yet do his meetness
And sovran sweetness
Hold in the jocund purpose of May.

So take your pleasure,
And in full measure
Use of your treasure,
When birds sing best!
For when heaven's bluest,
And earth feels newest,
And love longs truest,
And takes not rest:
When winds blow cleanest,
And seas roll sheenest,
And lawns lie greenest:
Then, night and day,
Dear life counts dearest,
And God walks nearest
To them that praise Him, praising His May.

XIII
I talked one midnight with the jolly ghost
Of a gray ancestor, TOM HEYWOOD hight;
And, 'Here's,' says he, his old heart liquor-lifted
'Here's how we did when GLORIANA shone:'

All in a garden green
Thrushes were singing;
Red rose and white between,
Lilies were springing;
It was the merry May;
Yet sang my Lady:
'Nay, Sweet, now nay, now nay!
I am not ready.'

Then to a pleasant shade
I did invite her:
All things a concert made,
For to delight her;
Under, the grass was gay;
Yet sang my Lady:
'Nay, Sweet, now nay, now nay!
I am not ready.'

XIV
Why do you linger and loiter, O most sweet?
Why do you falter and delay,
Now that the insolent, high-blooded May
Comes greeting and to greet?
Comes with her instant summonings to stray
Down the green, antient way
The leafy, still, rose-haunted, eye-proof street!
Where true lovers each other may entreat,
Ere the gold hair turn gray?
Entreat, and fleet
Life gaudily, and so play out their play,
Even with the triumphing May
The young-eyed, smiling, irresistible May!

Why do you loiter and linger, O most dear?
Why do you dream and palter and stay,
When every dawn, that rushes up the bay,
Brings nearer, and more near,
The Terror, the Discomforter, whose prey,
Beloved, we must be? Nor prayer, nor tear,
Lets his arraignment; but we disappear,
What time the gold turns gray,
Into the sheer,
Blind gulfs unglutted of mere Yesterday,
With the unlingering May
The good, fulfilling, irresponsible May!

XV

Come where my Lady lies,
Sleeping down the golden hours!
Cover her with flowers.

Bluebells from the clearings,
Flag-flowers from the rills,
Wildings from the lush hedgerows,
Delicate daffodils,
Sweetlings from the formal plots,
Bloomkins from the bowers
Heap them round her where she sleeps,
Cover her with flowers!

Sweet-pea and pansy,
Red hawthorn and white;
Gilliflowers like praising souls;
Lilies lamps of light:
Nurselings of what happy winds,
Suns, and stars, and showers!
Joylets good to see and smell
Cover her with flowers!

Like to sky-born shadows
Mirrored on a stream,
Let their odours meet and mix
And waver through her dream!
Last, the crowded sweetness
Slumber overpowers,
And she feels the lips she loves
Craving through the flowers!

XVI

The west a glory of green and red and gold,
The magical drifts to north and eastward rolled,
The shining sands, the still, transfigured sea,
The wind so light it scarce begins to be,
As these long days unfold a flower, unfold
Life's rose in me.

Life's rose life's rose! Red at my heart it glows
Glows and is glad, as in some quiet close
The sun's spoiled darlings their gay life renew!
Only, the clement rain, the mothering dew,
Daytide and night, all things that make the rose,
Are you, dear you!

XVII

Look down, dear eyes, look down,
Lest you betray her gladness.

Dear brows, do naught but frown,
Lest men miscall my madness.

Come not, dear hands, so near,
Lest all besides come nearer.
Dear heart, hold me less dear,
Lest time hold nothing dearer.

Keep me, dear lips, O, keep
The great last word unspoken,
Lest other eyes go weep,
And other lives lie broken!

XVIII
Poplar and lime and chestnut
Meet in a living screen;
And there the winds and the sunbeams keep
A revel of gold and green.

O, the green dreams and the golden,
The golden thoughts and green,
This green and golden end of May
My lover and me between!

XIX
Hither, this solemn eventide,
All flushed and mystical and blue,
When the late bird sings
And sweet-breathed garden-ghosts walk sudden and wide,
Hesper, that bringeth all good things,
Brings me a dream of you.
And in my heart, dear heart, it comes and goes,
Even as the south wind lingers and falls and blows,
Even as the south wind sighs and tarries and streams,
Among the living leaves about and round;
With a still, soothing sound,
As of a multitude of dreams
Of love, and the longing of love, and love's delight,
Thronging, ten thousand deep,
Into the uncreating Night,
With semblances and shadows to fulfil,
Amaze, and thrill
The strange, dispeopled silences of Sleep.

XX
After the grim daylight,
Night
Night and the stars and the sea!
Only the sea, and the stars
And the star-shown sails and spars
Naught else in the night for me!

Over the northern height,
Light
Light and the dawn of a day
With nothing for me but a breast
Laboured with love's unrest,
And the irk of an idle May!

XXI
Love, which is lust, is the Lamp in the Tomb.
Love, which is lust, is the Call from the Gloom.

Love, which is lust, is the Main of Desire.
Love, which is lust, is the Centric Fire.

So man and woman will keep their trust,
Till the very Springs of the Sea run dust.

Yea, each with the other will lose and win,
Till the very Sides of the Grave fall in.

For the strife of Love's the abysmal strife,
And the word of Love is the Word of Life.

And they that go with the Word unsaid,
Though they seem of the living, are damned and dead.

XXII
Between the dusk of a summer night
And the dawn of a summer day,
We caught at a mood as it passed in flight,
And we bade it stoop and stay.
And what with the dawn of night began
With the dusk of day was done;
For that is the way of woman and man,
When a hazard has made them one.

Arc upon arc, from shade to shine,
The World went thundering free;
And what was his errand but hers and mine
The lords of him, I and she?
O, it's die we must, but it's live we can,
And the marvel of earth and sun
Is all for the joy of woman and man
And the longing that makes them one.

XXIII
I took a hansom on to-day
For a round I used to know
That I used to take for a woman's sake
In a fever of to-and-fro.

There were the landmarks one and all
What did they stand to show?
Street and square and river were there
Where was the antient woe?

Never a hint of a challenging hope
Nor a hope laid sick and low,
But a longing dead as its kindred sped
A thousand years ago!

XXIV
Only a freakish wisp of hair?
Nay, but its wildest, its most frolic whorl
Stands for a slim, enamoured, sweet-fleshed girl!
And so, a tangle of dream and charm and fun,
Its every crook a promise and a snare,
Its every dowle, or genially gadding
Or crisply curled,
Heartening and madding,
Empales a novel and peculiar world
Of right, essential fantasies,
And shining acts as yet undone,
But in these wonder-working days
Soon, soon to ask our sovran Lord, the Sun,
For countenance and praise,
As of the best his storying eye hath seen,
And his vast memory can parallel,
Among the darling victories
Beneficent, beautiful, inexpressible
Of life on time!
Yet have they flashed and been
In millions, since 'twas his to bring
The heaven-creating Spring,
An angel of adventure and delight,
In all her beauty and all her strength and worth,
With her great guerdons of romance and spright,
And those high needs that fill the flesh with might,
Home to the citizens of this good, green earth.

Poor souls they have but time and place
To play their transient little play
And sing their singular little song,
Ere they are rushed away
Into the antient, undisclosing Night;
And none is left to tell of the clear eyes
That filled them with God's grace,
And turned the iron skies to skies of gold!
None; but the sweetest She herself grows old
Grows old, and dies;
And, but for such a lovely snatch of hair

As this, none, none could guess, or know
That She was kind and fair,
And he had nights and days beyond compare
How many dusty and silent years ago!

XXV
This is the moon of roses,
The lovely and flowerful time;
And, as white roses climb the wall,
Your dreams about me climb.

This is the moon of roses,
Glad and golden and blue;
And, as red roses drink of the sun,
My dreams they drink of you.

This is the moon of roses!
The cherishing South-West blows,
And life, dear heart, for me and you,
O, life's a rejoicing rose.

XXVI
June, and a warm, sweet rain;
June, and the call of a bird:
To a lover in pain
What lovelier word?

Two of each other fain
Happily heart on heart:
So in the wind and rain
Spring bears his part!

O, to be heart on heart
One with the warm June rain,
God with us from the start,
And no more pain!

XXVII
It was a bowl of roses:
There in the light they lay,
Languishing, glorying, glowing
Their life away.

And the soul of them rose like a presence,
Into me crept and grew,
And filled me with something, some one
O, was it you?

XXVIII
Your feet as glad
And light as a dove's homing wings, you came

Came with your sweets to fill my hands,
My sense with your perfume.

We closed with lips
Grown weary and fain with longing from afar,
The while your grave, enamoured eyes
Drank down the dream in mine.

Till the great need
So lovely and so instant grew, it seemed
The embodied Spirit of the Spring
Hung at me, heart on heart.

XXIX
A world of leafage murmurous and a-twinkle;
The green, delicious plenitude of June;
Love and laughter and song
The blue day long
Going to the same glad, golden tune
The same glad tune!

Clouds on the dim, delighting skies a-sprinkle;
Poplars black in the wake of a setting moon;
Love and languor and sleep
And the star-sown deep
Going to the same good, golden tune
The same good tune!

XXX
I send you roses, red, like love,
And white, like death, sweet friend:
Born in your bosom to rejoice,
Languish, and droop, and end.

If the white roses tell of death,
Let the red roses mend
The talk with true stories of love
Unchanging till the end.

Red and white roses, love and death
What else is left to send?
For what is life but love, the means,
And death, true Wife, the end?

XXXI
These glad, these great, these goodly days
Bewildering hope, outrunning praise,
The Earth, renewed by the great Sun's longing,
Utters her joy in a million ways!

What is there left, sweet Soul and true

What, for us and our dream to do?
What but to take this mighty Summer
As it were made for me and you?

Take it and live it beam by beam,
Motes of light on a gleaming stream,
Glare by glare and glory on glory
Through to the ash of this flaming dream!

XXXII
The downs, like uplands in Eden,
Gleam in an afterglow
Like a rose-world ruining earthwards
Mystical, wistful, slow!

Near and afar in the leafage,
That last glad call to the nest!
And the thought of you hangs and triumphs
With Hesper low in the west!

Till the song and the light and the colour,
The passion of earth and sky,
Are blent in a rapture of boding
Of the death we should one day die.

XXXIII
The time of the silence
Of birds is upon us:
Rust in the chestnut leaf,
Dust in the stubble:
The turn of the Year
And the call to decay.

Stately and splendid,
The Summer passes:
Sad with satiety,
Sick with fulfilment;
Spent and consumed,
But august till the end.

By wilting hedgerows
And white-hot highways,
Bearing its memories
Even as a burden,
The tired heart plods
For a place of rest.

XXXIV
There was no kiss that day?
No intimate Yea-and-Nay,
No sweets in hand, no tender, lingering touch?

None of those desperate, exquisite caresses,
So instant O, so brief! and yet so much,
The thought of the swiftest lifts and blesses?
Nor any one of those great royal words,
Those sovran privacies of speech,
Frank as the call of April birds,
That, whispered, live a life of gold
Among the heart's still sainted memories,
And irk, and thrill, and ravish, and beseech,
Even when the dream of dreams in death's a-cold?
No, there was none of these,
Dear one, and yet
O, eyes on eyes! O, voices breaking still,
For all the watchful will,
Into a kinder kindness than seemed due
From you to me, and me to you!
And that hot-eyed, close-throated, blind regret
Of woman and man baulked and debarred the blue!
No kiss, no kiss that day?
Nay, rather, though we seemed to wear the rue,
Sweet friend, how many, and how goodly say!

XXXV
Sing to me, sing, and sing again,
My glad, great-throated nightingale:
Sing, as the good sun through the rain
Sing, as the home-wind in the sail!

Sing to me life, and toil, and time,
O bugle of dawn, O flute of rest!
Sing, and once more, as in the prime,
There shall be naught but seems the best.

And sing me at the last of love:
Sing that old magic of the May,
That makes the great world laugh and move
As lightly as our dream to-day!

XXXVI
We sat late, late, talking of many things.
He told me of his grief, and, in the telling,
The gist of his tale showed to me, rhymed, like this.

It came, the news, like a fire in the night,
That life and its best were done;
And there was never so dazed a wretch
In the beat of the living sun.

I read the news, and the terms of the news
Reeled random round my brain
Like the senseless, tedious buzzle and boom

Of a bluefly in the pane.

So I went for the news to the house of the news,
But the words were left unsaid,
For the face of the house was blank with blinds,
And I knew that she was dead.

XXXVII
'Twas in a world of living leaves
That we two reaped and bound our sheaves:
They were of white roses and red,
And in the scything they were dead.

Now the high Autumn flames afield,
And what is all his golden yield
To that we took, and sheaved, and bound
In the green dusk that gladdened round?

Yet must the memory grieve and ache
Of that we did for dear love's sake,
But may no more under the sun,
Being, like our summer, spent and done.

XXXVIII
Since those we love and those we hate,
With all things mean and all things great,
Pass in a desperate disarray
Over the hills and far away:

It must be, Dear, that, late or soon,
Out of the ken of the watching moon,
We shall abscond with Yesterday
Over the hills and far away.

What does it matter? As I deem,
We shall but follow as brave a dream
As ever smiled a wanton May
Over the hills and far away.

We shall remember, and, in pride,
Fare forth, fulfilled and satisfied,
Into the land of Ever-and-Aye,
Over the hills and far away.

XXXIX
These were the woods of wonder
We found so close and boon,
When the bride-month in her beauty
Lay mouth to mouth with June.

November, the old, lean widow,

Sniffs, and snivels, and shrills,
And the bowers are all dismantled,
And the long grass wets and chills;

And I hate these dismal dawnings,
These miserable even-ends,
These orts, and rags, and heeltaps
This dream of being merely friends.

XL
'Dearest, when I am dead,
Make one last song for me:
Sing what I would have said
Righting life's wrong for me.

'Tell them how, early and late,
Glad ran the days with me,
Seeing how goodly and great,
Love, were your ways with me.'

XLI
Dear hands, so many times so much
When the spent year was green and prime,
Come, take your fill, and touch
This one poor time.

Dear lips, that could not leave unsaid
One sweet-souled syllable of delight,
Once more and be as dead
In the dead night.

Dear eyes, so fond to read in mine
The message of our counted years,
Look your proud last, nor shine
Through tears, through tears.

XLII
When, in what other life,
Where in what old, spent star,
Systems ago, dead vastitudes afar,
Were we two bird and bough, or man and wife?
Or wave and spar?
Or I the beating sea, and you the bar
On which it breaks? I know not, I!
But this, O this, my Very Dear, I know:
Your voice awakes old echoes in my heart;
And things I say to you now are said once more;
And, Sweet, when we two part,
I feel I have seen you falter and linger so,
So hesitate, and turn, and cling, yet go,
As once in some immemorable Before,

Once on some fortunate yet thrice-blasted shore.
Was it for good?
O, these poor eyes are wet;
And yet, O, yet,
Now that we know, I would not, if I could,
Forget.

XLIII
The rain and the wind, the wind and the rain
They are with us like a disease:
They worry the heart, they work the brain,
As they shoulder and clutch at the shrieking pane,
And savage the helpless trees.

What does it profit a man to know
These tattered and tumbling skies
A million stately stars will show,
And the ruining grace of the after-glow
And the rush of the wild sunrise?

Ever the rain, the rain and the wind!
Come, hunch with me over the fire,
Dream of the dreams that leered and grinned,
Ere the blood of the Year got chilled and thinned,
And the death came on desire!

XLIV
He made this gracious Earth a hell
With Love and Drink. I cannot tell
Of which he died. But Death was well.

Will I die of drink?
Why not?
Won't I pause and think?
What?
Why in seeming wise
Waste your breath?
Everybody dies
And of death!

Youth, if you find it's youth
Too late?
Truth and the back of truth?
Straight,
Be it love or liquor,
What's the odds,
So it slide you quicker
To the gods?

XLV
O, these long nights of days!

All the year's baseness in the ways,
All the year's wretchedness in the skies;
While on the blind, disheartened sea
A tramp-wind plies
Cringingly and dejectedly!
And rain and darkness, mist and mud,
They cling, they close, they sneak into the blood,
They crawl and crowd upon the brain:
Till in a dull, dense monotone of pain
The past is found a kind of maze,
At whose every coign and crook,
Broad angle and privy nook,
There waits a hooded Memory,
Sad, yet with strange, bright, unreproaching eyes.

XLVI
In Shoreham River, hurrying down
To the live sea,
By working, marrying, breeding Shoreham Town,
Breaking the sunset's wistful and solemn dream,
An old, black rotter of a boat
Past service to the labouring, tumbling flote,
Lay stranded in mid-stream:
With a horrid list, a frightening lapse from the line,
That made me think of legs and a broken spine:
Soon, all-too soon,
Ungainly and forlorn to lie
Full in the eye
Of the cynical, discomfortable moon
That, as I looked, stared from the fading sky,
A clown's face flour'd for work. And by and by
The wide-winged sunset wanned and waned;
The lean night-wind crept westward, chilling and sighing;
The poor old hulk remained,
Stuck helpless in mid-ebb. And I knew why
Why, as I looked, my heart felt crying.
For, as I looked, the good green earth seemed dying
Dying or dead;
And, as I looked on the old boat, I said:
'Dear God, it's I!'

XLVII
Come by my bed,
What time the gray ghost shrieks and flies;
Take in your hands my head,
And look, O look, into my failing eyes;
And, by God's grace,
Even as He sunders body and breath,
The shadow of your face
Shall pass with me into the run
Of the Beyond, and I shall keep and save

Your beauty, as it used to be,
An absolute part of me,
Lying there, dead and done,
Far from the sovran bounty of the sun,
Down in the grisly colonies of the Grave.

XLVIII
Gray hills, gray skies, gray lights,
And still, gray sea
O fond, O fair,
The Mays that were,
When the wild days and wilder nights
Made it like heaven to be!

Gray head, gray heart, gray dreams
O, breath by breath,
Night-tide and day
Lapse gentle and gray,
As to a murmur of tired streams,
Into the haze of death.

XLIX
Silence, loneliness, darkness
These, and of these my fill,
While God in the rush of the Maytide
Without is working His will.

Without are the wind and the wall-flowers,
The leaves and the nests and the rain,
And in all of them God is making
His beautiful purpose plain.

But I wait in a horror of strangeness
A tool on His workshop floor,
Worn to the butt, and banished
His hand for evermore.

L
So let me hence as one
Whose part in the world has been dreamed out and done:
One that hath fairly earned and spent
In pride of heart and jubilance of blood
Such wages, be they counted bad or good,
As Time, the old taskmaster, was moved to pay;
And, having warred and suffered, and passed on
Those gifts the Arbiters preferred and gave,
Fare, grateful and content,
Down the dim way
Whereby races innumerable have gone,
Into the silent universe of the grave.

Grateful for what hath been
For what my hand hath done, mine eyes have seen,
My heart been privileged to know;
With all my lips in love have brought
To lips that yearned in love to them, and wrought
In the way of wrath, and pity, and sport, and song:
Content, this miracle of being alive
Dwindling, that I, thrice weary of worst and best,
May shed my duds, and go
From right and wrong,
And, ceasing to regret, and long, and strive,
Accept the past, and be for ever at rest.

FINALE
Schizzando ma con sentimento

A sigh sent wrong,
A kiss that goes astray,
A sorrow the years endlong
So they say.

So let it be
Come the sorrow, the kiss, the sigh!
They are life, dear life, all three,
And we die.

WORTHING, 1899-1901.

LONDON TYPES
(To S. S. P.)

I. BUS-DRIVER
He's called The General from the brazen craft
And dash with which he sneaks a bit of road
And all its fares; challenged, or chafed, or chaffed,
Back-answers of the newest he'll explode;
He reins his horses with an air; he treats
With scoffing calm whatever powers there be;
He gets it straight, puts a bit on, and meets
His losses with both lip and pounds s. d.;
He arrogates a special taste in short;
Is loftily grateful for a flagrant smoke;
At all the smarter housemaids winks his court,
And taps them for half-crowns; being stoney-broke,
Lives lustily; is ever on the make;
And hath, I fear, none other gods but Fake.

II. LIFE-GUARDSMAN

Joy of the Milliner, Envy of the Line,
Star of the Parks, jack-booted, sworded, helmed,
He sits between his holsters, solid of spine;
Nor, as it seems, though WESTMINSTER were whelmed,
With the great globe, in earthquake and eclipse,
Would he and his charger cease from mounting guard,
This Private in the Blues, nor would his lips
Move, though his gorge with throttled oaths were charred!
He wears his inches weightily, as he wears
His old-world armours; and with his port and pride,
His sturdy graces and enormous airs,
He towers, in speech his Colonel countrified,
A triumph, waxing statelier year by year,
Of British blood, and bone, and beef, and beer.

III. HAWKER

Far out of bounds he's figured in a race
Of West-End traffic pitching to his loss.
But if you'd see him in his proper place,
Making the browns for bub and grub and doss,
Go East among the merchants and their men,
And where the press is noisiest, and the tides
Of trade run highest and widest, there and then
You shall behold him, edging with equal strides
Along the kerb; hawking in either hand
Some artful nothing made of twine and tin,
Cardboard and foil and bits of rubber band:
Some penn'orth of wit-in-fact that, with a grin,
The careful City marvels at, and buys
For nurselings in the Suburbs to despise!

IV. BEEF-EATER

His beat lies knee-high through a dust of story
A dust of terror and torture, grief and crime;
Ghosts that are ENGLAND'S wonder, and shame, and glory
Throng where he walks, an antic of old time;
A sense of long immedicable tears
Were ever with him, could his ears but heed;
The stern Hic Jacets of our bloodiest years
Are for his reading, had he eyes to read,
But here, where CROOKBACK raged, and CRANMER trimmed,
And MORE and STRAFFORD faced the axe's proving,
He shows that Crown the desperate Colonel nimmed,
Or simply keeps the Country Cousin moving,
Or stays such Cockney pencillers as would shame
The wall where some dead Queen hath traced her name.

V. SANDWICH-MAN

An ill March noon; the flagstones gray with dust;
An all-round east wind volleying straws and grit;
ST. MARTIN'S STEPS, where every venomous gust
Lingers to buffet, or sneap, the passing cit;
And in the gutter, squelching a rotten boot,
Draped in a wrap that, modish ten-year syne,
Partners, obscene with sweat and grease and soot,
A horrible hat, that once was just as fine;
The drunkard's mouth a-wash for something drinkable,
The drunkard's eye alert for casual toppers,
The drunkard's neck stooped to a lot scarce thinkable,
A living, crawling blazoning of Hot-Coppers,
He trails his mildews towards a Kingdom-Come
Compact of sausage-and-mash and two-o'-rum!

VI. 'LIZA

'LIZA'S old man's perhaps a little shady,
'LIZA'S old woman's prone to booze and cringe;
But 'LIZA deems herself a perfect lady,
And proves it in her feathers and her fringe.
For 'LIZA has a bloke her heart to cheer,
With pearlies and a barrer and a jack,
So all the vegetables of the year
Are duly represented on her back.
Her boots are sacrifices to her hats,
Which knock you speechless like a load of bricks!
Her summer velvets dazzle WANSTEAD FLATS,
And cost, at times, a good eighteen-and-six.
Withal, outside the gay and giddy whirl,
'LIZA'S a stupid, straight, hard-working girl.

VII. 'LADY'

Time, the old humourist, has a trick to-day
Of moving landmarks and of levelling down,
Till into Town the Suburbs edge their way,
And in the Suburbs you may scent the Town.
With MOUNT ST. thus approaching MUSWELL HILL,
And CLAPHAM COMMON marching with the MILE,
You get a HAMMERSMITH that fills the bill,
A HAMPSTEAD with a serious sense of style.
So this fair creature, pictured in THE ROW,
As one of that 'gay adulterous world,' {79} whose round
Is by the SERPENTINE, as well would show,
And might, I deem, as readily be found
On STREATHAM'S HILL, or WIMBLEDON'S, or where
Brixtonian kitchens lard the late-dining air.

VIII. BLUECOAT BOY

So went our boys when EDWARD SIXTH, the King,
Chartered CHRIST'S HOSPITAL, and died. And so
Full fifteen generations in a string
Of heirs to his bequest have had to go.
Thus CAMDEN showed, and BARNES, and STILLING-FLEET,
And RICHARDSON, that bade our LOVELACE be;
The little ELIA thus in NEWGATE STREET;
Thus to his GENEVIEVE young S. T. C.
With thousands else that, wandering up and down,
Quaint, privileged, liked and reputed well,
Made the great School a part of LONDON TOWN
Patent as PAUL'S and vital as BOW BELL:
The old School nearing exile, day by day,
To certain clay-lands somewhere HORSHAM way.

IX. MOUNTED POLICE

Army Reserve; a worshipper of BOBS,
With whom he stripped the smock from CANDAHAR;
Neat as his mount, that neatest among cobs;
Whenever pageants pass, or meetings are,
He moves conspicuous, vigilant, severe,
With his Light Cavalry hand and seat and look,
A living type of Order, in whose sphere
Is room for neither Hooligan nor Hook.
For in his shadow, wheresoe'er he ride,
Paces, all eye and hardihood and grip,
The dreaded Crusher, might in his every stride
And right materialized girt at his hip;
And they, that shake to see these twain go by,
Feel that the Tec, that plain-clothes Terror, is nigh.

X. NEWS-BOY

Take any station, pavement, circus, corner,
Where men their styles of print may call or choose,
And there, ten times more on it than JACK HORNER
There shall you find him swathed in sheets of news.
Nothing can stay the placing of his wares
Not bus, nor cab, nor dray! The very Slop,
That imp of power, is powerless! Ever he dares,
And, daring, lands his public neck and crop.
Even the many-tortured London ear,
The much-enduring, loathes his Speeshul yell,
His shriek of Winnur! But his dart and leer
And poise are irresistible. PALL MALL
Joys in him, and MILE END; for his vocation
Is to purvey the stuff of conversation.

XI. DRUM-MAJOR

Who says Drum-Major says a man of mould,
Shaking the meek earth with tremendous tread,
And pacing still, a triumph to behold,
Of his own spine at least two yards ahead!
Attorney, grocer, surgeon, broker, duke
His calling may be anything, who comes
Into a room, his presence a rebuke
To the dejected, as the pipes and drums
Inspired his port! who mounts his office stairs
As though he led great armies to the fight!
His bulk itself's pure genius, and he wears
His avoirdupois with so much fire and spright
That, though the creature stands but five feet five,
You take him for the tallest He alive.

XII. FLOWER-GIRL

There's never a delicate nurseling of the year
But our huge LONDON hails it, and delights
To wear it on her breast or at her ear,
Her days to colour and make sweet her nights.
Crocus and daffodil and violet,
Pink, primrose, valley-lily, clove-carnation,
Red rose and white rose, wall-flower, mignonette,
The daisies all these be her recreation,
Her gaudies these! And forth from DRURY LANE,
Trapesing in any of her whirl of weathers,
Her flower-girls foot it, honest and hoarse and vain,
All boot and little shawl and wilted feathers:
Of populous corners right advantage taking,
And, where they squat, endlessly posy-making.

XIII. BARMAID

Though, if you ask her name, she says ELISE,
Being plain ELIZABETH, e'en let it pass,
And own that, if her aspirates take their ease,
She ever makes a point, in washing glass,
Handling the engine, turning taps for tots,
And countering change, and scorning what men say,
Of posing as a dove among the pots,
Nor often gives her dignity away.
Her head's a work of art, and, if her eyes
Be tired and ignorant, she has a waist;
Cheaply the Mode she shadows; and she tries
From penny novels to amend her taste;
And, having mopped the zinc for certain years,
And faced the gas, she fades and disappears.
The Artist muses at his ease,
Contented that his work is done,

And smiling, smiling! as he sees
His crowd collecting, one by one.
Alas! his travail's but begun!
None, none can keep the years in line,
And what to Ninety-Eight is fun
May raise the gorge of Ninety-Nine!

MUSWELL HILL, 1898.

I. BEAU AUSTIN
By W. E. Henley and R. L. Stevenson,
Haymarket Theatre, November 3, 1890.

Spoken by Mr. TREE in the character of Beau Austin.

'To all and singular,' as DRYDEN says,
We bring a fancy of those Georgian days,
Whose style still breathed a faint and fine perfume
Of old-world courtliness and old-world bloom:
When speech was elegant and talk was fit,
For slang had not been canonised as wit;
When manners reigned, when breeding had the wall,
And Women, yes! were ladies first of all;
When Grace was conscious of its gracefulness,
And man, though Man! was not ashamed to dress.
A brave formality, a measured ease
Were his and hers, whose effort was to please.
And to excel in pleasing was to reign,
And, if you sighed, never to sigh in vain.

But then, as now, it may be, something more
Woman and man were human to the core.
The hearts that throbbed behind that brave attire
Burned with a plenitude of essential fire.
They too could risk, they also could rebel:
They could love wisely, they could love too well.
In that great duel of Sex, that ancient strife
Which is the very central fact of life,
They could, and did, engage it breath for breath,
They could, and did, get wounded unto death.
As at all times since time for us began
Woman was truly woman, man was man,
And joy and sorrow were as much at home
In trifling TUNBRIDGE as in mighty ROME.

Dead, dead and done with! Swift from shine to shade

The roaring generations flit and fade.
To this one, fading, flitting, like the rest,
We come to proffer, be it worst or best
A sketch, a shadow, of one brave old time;
A hint of what it might have held sublime;
A dream, an idyll, call it what you will,
Of man still Man, and woman. Woman still!

II. RICHARD SAVAGE
By J. M. Barrie and H. B. Marriott Watson, Criterion Theatre, April 16, 1891.

To other boards for pun and song and dance!
Our purpose is an essay in romance:
An old-world story where such old-world facts
As hate and love and death, through four swift acts
Not without gleams and glances, hints and cues,
From the dear bright eyes of the Comic Muse!
So shine and sound that, as we fondly deem,
They may persuade you to accept our dream:
Our own invention, mainly though we take,
Somewhat for art but most for interest's sake
One for our hero who goes wandering still
In the long shadow of PARNASSUS HILL;
Scarce within eyeshot; but his tragic shade
Compels that recognition due be made,
When he comes knocking at the student's door,
Something as poet, if as blackguard more.

Poet and blackguard. Of the first, how much?
As to the second, in quite perfect touch
With folly and sorrow, even shame and crime,
He lived the grief and wonder of his time!
Marked for reproaches from his life's beginning;
Extremely sinned against as well as sinning;
Hack, spendthrift, starveling, duellist in turn;
Too cross to cherish yet too fierce to spurn;
Begrimed with ink or brave with wine and blood;
Spirit of fire and manikin of mud;
Now shining clear, now fain to starve and skulk;
Star of the cellar, pensioner of the bulk;
At once the child of passion and the slave;
Brawling his way to an unhonoured grave
That was DICK SAVAGE! Yet, ere his ghost we raise
For these more decent and less desperate days,
It may be well and seemly to reflect
That, howbeit of so prodigal a sect,
Since it was his to call until the end
Our greatest, wisest Englishman his friend,
'Twere all-too fatuous if we cursed and scorned
The strange, wild creature JOHNSON loved and mourned.

Nature is but the oyster. Art's the pearl:
Our DICK is neither sycophant nor churl.
Not as he was but as he might have been
Had the Unkind Gods been poets of the scene,
Fired with our fancy, shaped and tricked anew
To touch your hearts with love, your eyes with rue,
He stands or falls, ere he these boards depart,
Not as dead Nature but as living Art.

III. ADMIRAL GUINEA
By W. E. Henley and R. L. Stevenson,
Avenue Theatre, Monday, November 29, 1897.

Spoken by Miss ELIZABETH ROBINS.

Once was an Age, an Age of blood and gold,
An Age of shipmen scoundrelly and bold
BLACKBEARD and AVORY, SINGLETON, ROBERTS, KIDD:
An Age which seemed, the while it rolled its quid,
Brave with adventure and doubloons and crime,
Rum and the Ebony Trade: when, time on time,
Real Pirates, right Sea-Highwaymen, could mock
The carrion strung at EXECUTION DOCK;
And the trim Slaver, with her raking rig,
Her cloud of sails, her spars superb and trig,
Held, in a villainous ecstasy of gain,
Her musky course from BENIN to the MAIN,
And back again for niggers:
When, in fine,
Some thought that EDEN bloomed across the Line,
And some, like COWPER'S NEWTON, lived to tell
That through those parallels ran the road to Hell.

Once was a pair of Friends, who loved to chance
Their feet in any by-way of Romance:
They, like two vagabond schoolboys, unafraid
Of stark impossibilities, essayed
To make these Penitent and Impenitent Thieves,
These PEWS and GAUNTS, each man of them with his sheaves
Of humour, passion, cruelty, tyranny, life,
Fit shadows for the boards; till in the strife
Of dream with dream, their Slaver-Saint came true,
And their Blind Pirate, their resurgent PEW
(A figure of deadly farce in his new birth),
Tap-tapped his way from ORCUS back to earth;
And so, their Lover and his Lass made one,
In their best prose this Admiral here was done.

One of this Pair sleeps till the crack of doom

Where the great ocean-rollers plunge and boom:
The other waits and wonders what his Friend,
Dead now, and deaf, and silent, were the end
Revealed to his rare spirit, would find to say
If you, his lovers, loved him for this Play.

EPICEDIA
TWO DAYS
(February 15 - September 28, 1894)
To V. G.

That day we brought our Beautiful One to lie
In the green peace within your gates, he came
To give us greeting, boyish and kind and shy,
And, stricken as we were, we blessed his name:
Yet, like the Creature of Light that had been ours,
Soon of the sweet Earth disinherited,
He too must join, even with the Year's old flowers,
The unanswering generations of the Dead.
So stand we friends for you, who stood our friend
Through him that day; for now through him you know
That though where love was, love is till the end,
Love, turned of death to longing, like a foe,
Strikes: when the ruined heart goes forth to crave
Mercy of the high, austere, unpitying Grave.

IN MEMORIAM
THOMAS EDWARD BROWN
(Ob. October 30, 1897)

He looked half-parson and half-skipper: a quaint,
Beautiful blend, with blue eyes good to see,
And old-world whiskers. You found him cynic, saint,
Salt, humourist, Christian, poet; with a free,
Far-glancing, luminous utterance; and a heart
Large as ST. FRANCIS'S: withal a brain
Stored with experience, letters, fancy, art,
And scored with runes of human joy and pain.
Till six-and-sixty years he used his gift,
His gift unparalleled, of laughter and tears,
And left the world a high-piled, golden drift
Of verse: to grow more golden with the years,
Till the Great Silence fallen upon his ways
Break into song, and he that had Love have Praise.

IN MEMORIAM
GEORGE WARRINGTON STEEVENS
London, December 10, 1869.

Ladysmith, January 15, 1900.

We cheered you forth, brilliant and kind and brave.
Under your country's triumphing flag you fell.
It floats, true Heart, over no dearer grave
Brave and brilliant and kind, hail and farewell!

LAST POST

The day's high work is over and done,
And these no more will need the sun:
Blow, you bugles of ENGLAND, blow!
These are gone whither all must go,
Mightily gone from the field they won.
So in the workaday wear of battle,
Touched to glory with GOD'S own red,
Bear we our chosen to their bed.
Settle them lovingly where they fell,
In that good lap they loved so well;
And, their deliveries to the dear LORD said,
And the last desperate volleys ranged and sped,
Blow, you bugles of ENGLAND, blow
Over the camps of her beaten foe
Blow glory and pity to the victor Mother,
Sad, O, sad in her sacrificial dead!

Labour, and love, and strife, and mirth,
They gave their part in this goodly Earth
Blow, you bugles of ENGLAND, blow!
That her Name as a sun among stars might glow,
Till the dusk of Time, with honour and worth:
That, stung by the lust and the pain of battle,
The One Race ever might starkly spread,
And the One Flag eagle it overhead!
In a rapture of wrath and faith and pride,
Thus they felt it, and thus they died;
So to the Maker of homes, to the Giver of bread,
For whose dear sake their triumphing souls they shed,
Blow, you bugles of ENGLAND, blow,
Though you break the heart of her beaten foe,
Glory and praise to the everlasting Mother,
Glory and peace to her lovely and faithful dead!

IN MEMORIAM
REGINAE DILECTISSIMAE VICTORIAE
(May 24, 1819 - January 22, 1901)

Sceptre and orb and crown,
High ensigns of a sovranty containing
The beauty and strength and state of half a World,

Pass from her, and she fades
Into the old, inviolable peace.

I

She had been ours so long
She seemed a piece of ENGLAND: spirit and blood
And message ENGLAND'S self,
Home-coloured, ENGLAND in look and deed and dream;
Like the rich meadows and woods, the serene rivers,
And sea-charmed cliffs and beaches, that still bring
A rush of tender pride to the heart
That beats in ENGLAND'S airs to ENGLAND'S ends:
August, familiar, irremovable,
Like the good stars that shine
In the good skies that only ENGLAND knows:
So that we held it sure
GOD'S aim, GOD'S will, GOD'S way,
When Empire from her footstool, realm on realm,
Spread, even as from her notable womb
Sprang line on line of Kings;
For she was ENGLAND - ENGLAND and our Queen.

II

O, she was ours! And she had aimed
And known and done the best
And highest in time: greatly rejoiced,
Ruled greatly, greatly endured. Love had been hers,
And widowhood, glory and grief, increase
In wisdom and power and pride,
Dominion, honour, children, reverence:
So that, in peace and war
Innumerably victorious, she lay down
To die in a world renewed,
Cleared, in her luminous umbrage beautified
For Man, and changing fast
Into so gracious an inheritance
As Man had never dared
Imagine. Think, when she passed,
Think what a pageant of immortal acts,
Done in the unapproachable face
Of Time by the high, transcending human mind,
Shone and acclaimed
And triumphed in her advent! Think of the ghosts,
Think of the mighty ghosts: soldiers and priests,
Artists and captains of discovery,
GOD'S chosen, His adventurers up the heights
Of thought and deed, how many of them that led
The forlorn hopes of the World!
Her peers and servants, made the air
Of her death-chamber glorious! Think how they thronged
About her bed, and with what pride

They took this sister-ghost
Tenderly into the night! O, think
And, thinking, bow the head
In sorrow, but in the reverence that makes
The strong man stronger, this true maid,
True wife, true mother, tried and found
An hundred times true steel,
This unforgettable woman was your Queen!

III
Tears for her, tears! Tears and the mighty rites
Of an everlasting and immense farewell,
ENGLAND, green heart of the world, and you,
Dear demi-ENGLANDS, far-away isles of home,
Where the old speech is native, and the old flag
Floats, and the old irresistible call,
The watch-word of so many ages of years,
Makes men in love
With toil for the race, and pain, and peril, and death!
Tears, and the dread, tremendous dirge
Of her brooding battleships, and hosts
Processional, with trailing arms; the plaint
Measured, enormous, terrible of her guns;
The slow, heart-breaking throb
Of bells; the trouble of drums; the blare
Of mourning trumpets; the discomforting pomp
Of silent crowds, black streets, and banners-royal
Obsequious! Then, these high things done,
Rise, heartened of your passion! Rise to the height
Of her so lofty life! Kneel, if you must;
But, kneeling, win to those great altitudes
On which she sought and did
Her clear, supernal errand unperturbed!
Let the new memory
Be as the old, long love! So, when the hour
Strikes, as it must, for valour of heart,
Virtue, and patience, and unblenching hope,
And the inflexible resolve
That, come the World in arms,
This breeder of nations, ENGLAND, keeping the seas
Hers as from GOD, shall in the sight of GOD
Stand justified of herself
Wherever her unretreating bugles blow!
Remember that she lived
That this magnificent Power might still perdure
Your friend, your passionate servant, counsellor, Queen.

IV
Be that your chief of mourning that!
ENGLAND, O Mother, and you,
The daughter Kingdoms born and reared

Of ENGLAND'S travail and sweet blood;
And never will you lands,
The live Earth over and round,
Wherethrough for sixty royal and radiant years
Her drum-tap made the dawns
English. Never will you
So fittingly and well have paid your debt
Of grief and gratitude to the souls
That sink in ENGLAND'S harness into the dream:
'I die for ENGLAND'S sake, and it is well':
As now to this valiant, wonderful piece of earth,
To which the assembling nations bare the head,
And bend the knee,
In absolute veneration, once your Queen.

Sceptre and orb and crown,
High ensigns of a sovranty empaling
The glory and love and praise of a whole half-world,
Fall from her, and, preceding, she departs
Into the old, indissoluble Peace.

EPILOGUE
Into a land
Storm-wrought, a place of quakes, all thunder-scarred,
Helpless, degraded, desolate,
Peace, the White Angel, comes.
Her eyes are as a mother's. Her good hands
Are comforting, and helping; and her voice
Falls on the heart, as, after Winter, Spring
Falls on the World, and there is no more pain.
And, in her influence, hope returns, and life,
And the passion of endeavour: so that, soon,
The idle ports are insolent with keels;
The stithies roar, and the mills thrum
With energy and achievement; weald and wold
Exult; the cottage-garden teems
With innocent hues and odours; boy and girl
Mate prosperously; there are sweet women to kiss;
There are good women to breed. In a golden fog,
A large, full-stomached faith in kindliness
All over the world, the nation, in a dream
Of money and love and sport, hangs at the paps
Of well-being, and so
Goes fattening, mellowing, dozing, rotting down
Into a rich deliquium of decay.

Then, if the Gods be good,
Then, if the Gods be other than mischievous,
Down from their footstools, down
With a million-throated shouting, swoops and storms
War, the Red Angel, the Awakener,

The Shaker of Souls and Thrones; and at her heel
Trail grief, and ruin, and shame!
The woman weeps her man, the mother her son,
The tenderling its father. In wild hours,
A people, haggard with defeat,
Asks if there be a God; yet sets its teeth,
Faces calamity, and goes into the fire
Another than it was. And in wild hours
A people, roaring ripe
With victory, rises, menaces, stands renewed,
Sheds its old piddling aims,
Approves its virtue, puts behind itself
The comfortable dream, and goes,
Armoured and militant,
New-pithed, new-souled, new-visioned, up the steeps
To those great altitudes, whereat the weak
Live not. But only the strong
Have leave to strive, and suffer, and achieve.

WORTHING, 1901.

THE SONG OF THE SWORD
(To Rudyard Kipling)

The Sword
Singing
The voice of the Sword from the heart of the Sword
Clanging imperious
Forth from Time's battlements
His ancient and triumphing Song.

In the beginning,
Ere God inspired Himself
Into the clay thing
Thumbed to His image,
The vacant, the naked shell
Soon to be Man:
Thoughtful He pondered it,
Prone there and impotent,
Fragile, inviting
Attack and discomfiture:
Then, with a smile
As He heard in the Thunder
That laughed over Eden
The voice of the Trumpet,
The iron Beneficence,
Calling His dooms
To the Winds of the world
Stooping, He drew

On the sand with His finger
A shape for a sign
Of His way to the eyes
That in wonder should waken,
For a proof of His will
To the breaking intelligence:
That was the birth of me:
I am the Sword.

Hard and bleak, keen and cruel,
Short-hilted, long-shafted,
I froze into steel:
And the blood of my elder,
His hand on the hafts of me,
Sprang like a wave
In the wind, as the sense
Of his strength grew to ecstasy,
Glowed like a coal
At the throat of the furnace,
As he knew me and named me
The War-Thing, the Comrade,
Father of honour
And giver of kingship,
The fame-smith, the song-master,
Bringer of women
On fire at his hands
For the pride of fulfilment,
Priest (saith the Lord)
Of his marriage with victory.
Ho! then, the Trumpet,
Handmaid of heroes,
Calling the peers
To the place of espousal!
Ho! then, the splendour
And sheen of my ministry,
Clothing the earth
With a livery of lightnings!
Ho! then, the music
Of battles in onset
And ruining armours,
And God's gift returning
In fury to God!
Glittering and keen
As the song of the winter stars,
Ho! then, the sound
Of my voice, the implacable
Angel of Destiny!
I am the Sword.

Heroes, my children,
Follow, O follow me,

Follow, exulting
In the great light that breaks
From the sacred companionship:
Thrust through the fatuous,
Thrust through the fungous brood
Spawned in my shadow
And gross with my gift!
Thrust through, and hearken,
O hark, to the Trumpet,
The Virgin of Battles,
Calling, still calling you
Into the Presence,
Sons of the Judgment,
Pure wafts of the Will!
Edged to annihilate,
Hilted with government,
Follow, O follow me
Till the waste places
All the grey globe over
Ooze, as the honeycomb
Drips, with the sweetness
Distilled of my strength:
And, teeming in peace
Through the wrath of my coming,
They give back in beauty
The dread and the anguish
They had of me visitant!
Follow, O follow, then,
Heroes, my harvesters!
Where the tall grain is ripe
Thrust in your sickles:
Stripped and adust
In a stubble of empire,
Scything and binding
The full sheaves of sovranty:
Thus, O thus gloriously,
Shall you fulfil yourselves:
Thus, O thus mightily,
Show yourselves sons of mine
Yea, and win grace of me:
I am the Sword.

I am the feast-maker:
Hark, through a noise
Of the screaming of eagles,
Hark how the Trumpet,
The mistress of mistresses,
Calls, silver-throated
And stern, where the tables
Are spread, and the work
Of the Lord is in hand!

Driving the darkness,
Even as the banners
And spears of the Morning;
Sifting the nations,
The slag from the metal,
The waste and the weak
From the fit and the strong;
Fighting the brute,
The abysmal Fecundity;
Checking the gross,
Multitudinous blunders,
The groping, the purblind
Excesses in service,
Of the Womb universal,
The absolute Drudge;
Changing the charactry
Carved on the World,
The miraculous gem
In the seal-ring that burns
On the hand of the Master
Yea! and authority
Flames through the dim,
Unappeasable Grisliness
Prone down the nethermost
Chasms of the Void;
Clear singing, clean slicing;
Sweet spoken, soft finishing;
Making death beautiful,
Life but a coin
To be staked in the pastime
Whose playing is more
Than the transfer of being;
Arch-anarch, chief builder,
Prince and evangelist,
I am the Will of God:
I am the Sword.

The Sword
Singing
The voice of the Sword from the heart of the Sword
Clanging majestical,
As from the starry-staired
Courts of the primal Supremacy,
His high, irresistible song.

LONDON VOLUNTARIES
(To Charles Whibley)

I

Andante con mote

Forth from the dust and din,
The crush, the heat, the many-spotted glare,
The odour and sense of life and lust aflare,
The wrangle and jangle of unrests,
Let us take horse, dear heart, take horse and win
As from swart August to the green lap of May
To quietness and the fresh and fragrant breasts
Of the still, delicious night, not yet aware
In any of her innumerable nests
Of that first sudden plash of dawn,
Clear, sapphirine, luminous, large,
Which tells that soon the flowing springs of day
In deep and ever deeper eddies drawn
Forward and up, in wider and wider way
Shall float the sands and brim the shores
On this our haunch of Earth, as round she roars
And spins into the outlook of the Sun
(The Lord's first gift, the Lord's especial charge)
With light, with living light, from marge to marge,
Until the course He set and staked be run.

Through street and square, through square and street,
Each with his home-grown quality of dark
And violated silence, loud and fleet,
Waylaid by a merry ghost at every lamp,
The hansom wheels and plunges. Hark, O hark,
Sweet, how the old mare's bit and chain
Ring back a rough refrain
Upon the marked and cheerful tramp
Of her four shoes! Here is the Park,
And O the languid midsummer wafts adust,
The tired midsummer blooms!
O the mysterious distances, the glooms
Romantic, the august
And solemn shapes! At night this City of Trees
Tunis to a tryst of vague and strange
And monstrous Majesties,
Let loose from some dim underworld to range
These terrene vistas till their twilight sets:
When, dispossessed of wonderfulness, they stand
Beggared and common, plain to all the land
For stooks of leaves! And lo! the wizard hour
Whose shining, silent sorcery hath such power!
Still, still the streets, between their carcanets
Of linking gold, are avenues of sleep:
But see how gable ends and parapets
In gradual beauty and significance
Emerge! And did you hear
That little twitter-and-cheep,

Breaking inordinately loud and clear
On this still, spectral, exquisite atmosphere?
'Tis a first nest at matins! And behold
A rakehell cat, how furtive and acold!
A spent witch homing from some infamous dance
Obscene, quick-trotting, see her tip and fade
Through shadowy railings into a pit of shade!
And lo! a little wind and shy,
The smell of ships (that earnest of romance),
A sense of space and water, and thereby
A lamplit bridge ouching the troubled sky.
And look, O look! a tangle of silver gleams
And dusky lights, our River and all his dreams,
His dreams of a dead past that cannot die!

What miracle is happening in the air,
Charging the very texture of the gray
With something luminous and rare?
The night goes out like an ill-parcelled fire,
And, as one lights a candle, it is day.
The extinguisher that fain would strut for spire
On the formal little church is not yet green
Across the water: but the house-tops nigher,
The corner-lines, the chimneys, look how clean,
How new, how naked! See the batch of boats,
Here at the stairs, washed in the fresh-sprung beam!
And those are barges that were goblin floats,
Black, hag-steered, fraught with devilry and dream!
And in the piles the water frolics clear,
The ripples into loose rings wander and flee,
And we, we can behold that could but hear
The ancient River singing as he goes
New-mailed in morning to the ancient Sea.
The gas burns lank and jaded in its glass:
The old Ruffian soon shall yawn himself awake,
And light his pipe, and shoulder his tools, and take
His hobnailed way to work!
Let us too pass:
Through these long blindfold rows
Of casements staring blind to right and left,
Each with his gaze turned inward on some piece
Of life in death's own likeness. Life bereft
Of living looks as by the Great Release
(Perchance of shadow-shapes from shadow-shows),
Whose upshot all men know yet no man knows.

Reach upon reach of burial, so they feel,
These colonies of dreams! And as we steal
Homeward together, but for the buxom breeze
That frolics at our heel,
Greeting the town with news of the summer seas,

We might, thus awed, thus lonely that we are
Be wandering some depopulated star,
Some world of memories and unbroken graves,
So broods the abounding Silence near and far:
Till even your footfall craves
Forgiveness of the majesty it braves.

II
Scherzando

Down through the ancient Strand
The Spirit of October, mild and boon
And sauntering, takes his way
This golden end of afternoon,
As though the corn stood yellow in all the land
And the ripe apples dropped to the harvest-moon.

Lo! the round sun, half down the western slope
Seen as along an unglazed telescope
Lingers and lolls, loth to be done with day:
Gifting the long, lean, lanky street
And its abounding confluences of being
With aspects generous and bland:
Making a thousand harnesses to shine
As with new ore from some enchanted mine,
And every horse's coat so full of sheen
He looks new-tailored, and every 'bus feels clean,
And never a hansom but is worth the feeing;
And every jeweller within the pale
Offers a real Arabian Night for sale;
And even the roar
Of the strong streams of toil that pause and pour
Eastward and westward sounds suffused
Seems as it were bemused
And blurred, and like the speech
Of lazy seas upon a lotus-eating beach
With this enchanted lustrousness,
This mellow magic, that (as a man's caress
Brings back to some faded face beloved before
A heavenly shadow of the grace it wore
Ere the poor eyes were minded to beseech)
Old things transfigures, and you hail and bless
Their looks of long-lapsed loveliness once more;
Till the sedate and mannered elegance
Of Clement's is all tinctured with romance;
The while the fanciful, formal, finicking charm
Of Bride's, that madrigal in stone,
Glows flushed and warm
And beauteous with a beauty not its own;
And the high majesty of Paul's

Uplifts a voice of living light, and calls
Calls to his millions to behold and see
How goodly this his London Town can be!

For earth and sky and air
Are golden everywhere,
And golden with a gold so suave and fine
The looking on it lifts the heart like wine.
Trafalgar Square
(The fountains volleying golden glaze)
Gleams like an angel-market. High aloft
Over his couchant Lions in a haze
Shimmering and bland and soft,
A dust of chrysoprase,
Our Sailor takes the golden gaze
Of the saluting sun, and flames superb
As once he flamed it on his ocean round.
The dingy dreariness of the picture-place,
Turned very nearly bright,
Takes on a certain dismal grace,
And shows not all a scandal to the ground.
The very blind man pottering on the kerb,
Among the posies and the ostrich feathers
And the rude voices touched with all the weathers
Of all the varying year,
Shares in the universal alms of light.
The windows, with their fleeting, flickering fires,
The height and spread of frontage shining sheer,
The glistering signs, the rejoicing roofs and spires
'Tis El Dorado, El Dorado plain,
The Golden City! And when a girl goes by,
Look! as she turns her glancing head,
A call of gold is floated from her ear!
Golden, all golden! In a golden glory,
Long lapsing down a golden coasted sky,
The day not dies but seems
Dispersed in wafts and drifts of gold, and shed
Upon a past of golden song and story
And memories of gold and golden dreams.

III
Largo e mesto

Out of the poisonous East,
Over a continent of blight,
Like a maleficent Influence released
From the most squalid cellarage of hell,
The Wind-Fiend, the abominable
The hangman wind that tortures temper and light
Comes slouching, sullen and obscene,

Hard on the skirts of the embittered night:
And in a cloud unclean
Of excremental humours, roused to strife
By the operation of some ruinous change
Wherever his evil mandate run and range
Into a dire intensity of life,
A craftsman at his bench, he settles down
To the grim job of throttling London Town.

And, by a jealous lightlessness beset
That might have oppressed the dragons of old time
Crunching and groping in the abysmal slime,
A cave of cut-throat thoughts and villainous dreams,
Hag-rid and crying with cold and dirt and wet,
The afflicted city, prone from mark to mark
In shameful occultation, seems
A nightmare labyrinthine, dim and drifting,
With wavering gulfs and antic heights and shifting
Rent in the stuff of a material dark
Wherein the lamplight, scattered and sick and pale,
Shows like the leper's living blotch of bale:
Uncoiling monstrous into street on street
Paven with perils, teeming with mischance,
Where man and beast go blindfold and in dread,
Working with oaths and threats and faltering feet
Somewhither in the hideousness ahead;
Working through wicked airs and deadly dews
That make the laden robber grin askance
At the good places in his black romance,
And the poor, loitering harlot rather choose
Go pinched and pined to bed
Than lurk and shiver and curse her wretched way
From arch to arch, scouting some threepenny prey.

Forgot his dawns and far-flushed afterglows,
His green garlands and windy eyots forgot,
The old Father-River flows,
His watchfires cores of menace in the gloom,
As he came oozing from the Pit, and bore,
Sunk in his filthily transfigured sides,
Shoals of dishonoured dead to tumble and rot
In the squalor of the universal shore:
His voices sounding through the gruesome air
As from the ferry where the Boat of Doom
With her blaspheming cargo reels and rides:
The while his children, the brave ships,
No more adventurous and fair
Nor tripping it light of heel as home-bound brides,
But infamously enchanted,
Huddle together in the foul eclipse,
Or feel their course by inches desperately,

As through a tangle of alleys murder-haunted,
From sinister reach to reach – out – out to sea.

And Death the while
Death with his well-worn, lean, professional smile,
Death in his threadbare working trim
Comes to your bedside, unannounced and bland,
And with expert, inevitable hand
Feels at your windpipe, fingers you in the lung,
Or flicks the clot well into the labouring heart:
Thus signifying unto old and young,
However hard of mouth or wild of whim,
'Tis time 'tis time by his ancient watch to part
With books and women and talk and drink and art:
And you go humbly after him
To a mean suburban lodging: on the way
To what or where
Not Death, who is old and very wise, can say:
And you, how should you care
So long as, unreclaimed of hell,
The Wind-Fiend, the insufferable,
Thus vicious and thus patient sits him down
To the black job of burking London Town?

IV
Allegro maestoso

Spring winds that blow
As over leagues of myrtle-blooms and may;
Bevies of spring clouds trooping slow,
Like matrons heavy-bosomed and aglow
With the mild and placid pride of increase! Nay,
What makes this insolent and comely stream
Of appetence, this freshet of desire
(Milk from the wild breasts of the wilful Day!),
Down Piccadilly dance and murmur and gleam
In genial wave on wave and gyre on gyre?
Why does that nymph unparalleled splash and churn
The wealth of her enchanted urn
Till, over-billowing all between
Her cheerful margents grey and living green,
It floats and wanders, glittering and fleeing,
An estuary of the joy of being?
Why should the buxom leafage of the Park
Touch to an ecstasy the act of seeing?
As if my paramour, my bride of brides,
Lingering and flushed, mysteriously abides
In some dim, eye-proof angle of odorous dark,
Some smiling nook of green-and-golden shade,
In the divine conviction robed and crowned

The globe fulfils his immemorial round
But as the marrying-place of all things made!

There is no man, this deifying day,
But feels the primal blessing in his blood.
The sacred impulse of the May
Brightening like sex made sunshine through her veins,
There is no woman but disdains
To vail the ensigns of her womanhood.
None but, rejoicing, flaunts them as she goes,
Bounteous in looks of her delicious best,
On her inviolable quest:
These with their hopes, with their sweet secrets those,
But all desirable and frankly fair,
As each were keeping some most prosperous tryst,
And in the knowledge went imparadised.
For look! a magical influence everywhere,
Look how the liberal and transfiguring air
Washes this inn of memorable meetings,
This centre of ravishments and gracious greetings,
Till, through its jocund loveliness of length
A tidal-race of lust from shore to shore,
A brimming reach of beauty met with strength,
It shines and sounds like some miraculous dream,
Some vision multitudinous and agleam,
Of happiness as it shall be evermore!

Praise God for giving
Through this His messenger among the days
His word the life He gave is thrice-worth living!
For Pan, the bountiful, imperious Pan
Not dead, not dead, as dreamers feigned,
But the lush genius of a million Mays
Renewing his beneficent endeavour!
Still reigns and triumphs, as he hath triumphed and reigned
Since in the dim blue dawn of time
The universal ebb-and-flow began,
To sound his ancient music, and prevails
By the persuasion of his mighty rhyme
Here in this radiant and immortal street
Lavishly and omnipotently as ever
In the open hills, the undissembling dales,
The laughing-places of the juvenile earth.
For lo! the wills of man and woman meet,
Meet and are moved, each unto each endeared
As once in Eden's prodigal bowers befell,
To share his shameless, elemental mirth
In one great act of faith, while deep and strong,
Incomparably nerved and cheered,
The enormous heart of London joys to beat
To the measures of his rough, majestic song:

The lewd, perennial, overmastering spell
That keeps the rolling universe ensphered
And life and all for which life lives to long
Wanton and wondrous and for ever well.

RHYMES AND RHYTHMS
I

Where forlorn sunsets flare and fade
On desolate sea and lonely sand,
Out of the silence and the shade
What is the voice of strange command
Calling you still, as friend calls friend
With love that cannot brook delay,
To rise and follow the ways that wend
Over the hills and far away?

Hark in the city, street on street
A roaring reach of death and life,
Of vortices that clash and fleet
And ruin in appointed strife,
Hark to it calling, calling clear,
Calling until you cannot stay
From dearer things than your own most dear
Over the hills and far away.

Out of the sound of ebb and flow,
Out of the sight of lamp and star,
It calls you where the good winds blow,
And the unchanging meadows are:
From faded hopes and hopes agleam,
It calls you, calls you night and day
Beyond the dark into the dream
Over the hills and far away.

II
A desolate shore,
The sinister seduction of the Moon,
The menace of the irreclaimable Sea.

Flaunting, tawdry and grim,
From cloud to cloud along her beat,
Leering her battered and inveterate leer,
She signals where he prowls in the dark alone,
Her horrible old man,
Mumbling old oaths and warming
His villainous old bones with villainous talk
The secrets of their grisly housekeeping
Since they went out upon the pad

In the first twilight of self-conscious Time:
Growling, obscene and hoarse,
Tales of unnumbered Ships,
Goodly and strong, Companions of the Advance
In some vile alley of the night
Waylaid and bludgeoned
Dead.

Deep cellared in primeval ooze,
Ruined, dishonoured, spoiled,
They lie where the lean water-worm
Crawls free of their secrets, and their broken sides
Bulge with the slime of life. Thus they abide,
Thus fouled and desecrate,
The summons of the Trumpet, and the while
These Twain, their murderers,
Unravined, imperturbable, unsubdued,
Hang at the heels of their children. She aloft
As in the shining streets,
He as in ambush at some fetid stair.

The stalwart Ships,
The beautiful and bold adventurers!
Stationed out yonder in the isle,
The tall Policeman,
Flashing his bull's-eye, as he peers
About him in the ancient vacancy,
Tells them this way is safety, this way home.

III
(To R. F. B.)

We are the Choice of the Will: God, when He gave the word
That called us into line, set in our hand a sword;

Set us a sword to wield none else could lift and draw,
And bade us forth to the sound of the trumpet of the Law.

East and west and north, wherever the battle grew,
As men to a feast we fared, the work of the Will to do.

Bent upon vast beginnings, bidding anarchy cease
(Had we hacked it to the Pit, we had left it a place of peace!)

Marching, building, sailing, pillar of cloud or fire,
Sons of the Will, we fought the fight of the Will, our sire.

Road was never so rough that we left its purpose dark;
Stark was ever the sea, but our ships were yet more stark;

We tracked the winds of the world to the steps of their very thrones;
The secret parts of the world were salted with our bones;

Till now the name of names, England, the name of might,
Flames from the austral bounds to the ends of the northern night;

And the call of her morning drum goes in a girdle of sound,
Like the voice of the sun in song, the great globe round and round;

And the shadow of her flag, when it shouts to the mother-breeze,
Floats from shore to shore of the universal seas;

And the loneliest death is fair with a memory of her flowers,
And the end of the road to Hell with the sense of her dews and showers!

Who says that we shall pass, or the fame of us fade and die,
While the living stars fulfil their round in the living sky?

For the sire lives in his sons, and they pay their father's debt,
And the Lion has left a whelp wherever his claw was set:

And the Lion in his whelps, his whelps that none shall brave,
Is but less strong than Time and the all-devouring Grave.

IV

It came with the threat of a waning moon
And the wail of an ebbing tide,
But many a woman has lived for less,
And many a man has died;
For life upon life took hold and passed,
Strong in a fate set free,
Out of the deep, into the dark,
On for the years to be.

Between the gleam of a waning moon
And the song of an ebbing tide,
Chance upon chance of love and death
Took wing for the world so wide.
Leaf out of leaf is the way of the land,
Wave out of wave of the sea;
And who shall reckon what lives may live
In the life that we bade to be?

V

Why, my heart, do we love her so?
(Geraldine, Geraldine!)
Why does the great sea ebb and flow?

Why does the round world spin?
Geraldine, Geraldine,
Bid me my life renew,
What is it worth unless I win,
Love, love and you?

Why, my heart, when we speak her name
(Geraldine, Geraldine!),
Throbs the word like a flinging flame?
Why does the spring begin?
Geraldine, Geraldine,
Bid me indeed to be,
Open your heart and take us in,
Love, love and me.

VI

Space and dread and the dark
Over a livid stretch of sky
Cloud-monsters crawling like a funeral train
Of huge primeval presences
Stooping beneath the weight
Of some enormous, rudimentary grief;
While in the haunting loneliness
The far sea waits and wanders, with a sound
As of the trailing skirts of Destiny
Passing unseen
To some immitigable end
With her grey henchman, Death.

What larve, what spectre is this
Thrilling the wilderness to life
As with the bodily shape of Fear?
What but a desperate sense,
A strong foreboding of those dim,
Interminable continents, forlorn
And many-silenced in a dusk
Inviolable utterly, and dead
As the poor dead it huddles and swarms and styes
In hugger-mugger through eternity?

Life, life, let there be life!
Better a thousand times the roaring hours
When wave and wind,
Like the Arch-Murderer in flight
From the Avenger at his heel,
Storm through the desolate fastnesses
And wild waste places of the world!

Life, give me life until the end,

That at the very top of being,
The battle-spirit shouting in my blood,
Out of the reddest hell of the fight
I may be snatched and flung
Into the everlasting lull,
The immortal, incommunicable dream.

VII

There's a regret
So grinding, so immitigably sad,
Remorse thereby feels tolerant, even glad. . . .
Do you not know it yet?

For deeds undone
Rankle, and snarl, and hunger for their due
Till there seems naught so despicable as you
In all the grin o' the sun.

Like an old shoe
The sea spurns and the land abhors, you lie
About the beach of Time, till by-and-by
Death, that derides you too

Death, as he goes
His ragman's round, espies you, where you stray,
With half-an-eye, and kicks you out of his way;
And then and then, who knows

But the kind Grave
Turns on you, and you feel the convict Worm,
In that black bridewell working out his term,
Hanker and grope and crave?

'Poor fool that might
That might, yet would not, dared not, let this be,
Think of it, here and thus made over to me
In the implacable night!'

And writhing, fain
And like a lover, he his fill shall take
Where no triumphant memory lives to make
His obscene victory vain.

VIII
(To J. A. C.)

Fresh from his fastnesses
Wholesome and spacious,

The north wind, the mad huntsman,
Halloos on his white hounds
Over the grey, roaring
Reaches and ridges,
The forest of ocean,
The chace of the world.
Hark to the peal
Of the pack in full cry,
As he thongs them before him
Swarming voluminous,
Weltering, wide-wallowing,
Till in a ruining
Chaos of energy,
Hurled on their quarry,
They crash into foam!

Old Indefatigable,
Time's right-hand man, the sea
Laughs as in joy
From his millions of wrinkles:
Laughs that his destiny,
Great with the greatness
Of triumphing order,
Shows as a dwarf
By the strength of his heart
And the might of his hands.

Master of masters,
O maker of heroes,
Thunder the brave,
Irresistible message:
'Life is worth living
Through every grain of it
From the foundations
To the last edge
Of the cornerstone, death.'

IX

'As like the Woman as you can'
(Thus the New Adam was beguiled)
'So shall you touch the Perfect Man'
(God in the Garden heard and smiled).
'Your father perished with his day:
'A clot of passions fierce and blind
'He fought, he slew, he hacked his way:
'Your muscles, Child, must be of mind.

'The Brute that lurks and irks within,
'How, till you have him gagged and bound,

'Escape the foullest form of Sin?'
(God in the Garden laughed and frowned).
'So vile, so rank, the bestial mood
'In which the race is bid to be,
'It wrecks the Rarer Womanhood:
'Live, therefore, you, for Purity!

'Take for your mate no buxom croup,
'No girl all grace and natural will:
'To make her happy were to stoop
'From light to dark, from Good to Ill.
'Choose one of whom your grosser make'
(God in the Garden laughed outright)
'The true refining touch may take
'Till both attain Life's highest height.

'There, equal, purged of soul and sense,
'Beneficent, high-thinking, just,
'Beyond the appeal of Violence,
'Incapable of common Lust,
'In mental Marriage still prevail'
(God in the Garden hid His face)
'Till you achieve that Female-Male,
'In Which shall culminate the race.

X

Midsummer midnight skies,
Midsummer midnight influences and airs,
The shining sensitive silver of the sea
Touched with the strange-hued blazonings of dawn:
And all so solemnly still I seem to hear
The breathing of Life and Death,
The secular Accomplices,
Renewing the visible miracle of the world.

The wistful stars
Shine like good memories. The young morning wind
Blows full of unforgotten hours
As over a region of roses. Life and Death
Sound on, sound on. . . . And the night magical,
Troubled yet comforting, thrills
As if the Enchanted Castle at the heart
Of the wood's dark wonderment
Swung wide his valves and filled the dim sea-banks
With exquisite visitants:
Words fiery-hearted yet, dreams and desires
With living looks intolerable, regrets
Whose voice comes as the voice of an only child
Heard from the grave: shapes of a Might-Have-Been

Beautiful, miserable, distraught
The Law no man may baffle denied and slew.

The spell-bound ships stand as at gaze
To let the marvel by. The grey road glooms . . .
Glimmers . . . goes out . . . and there, O there where it fades,
What grace, what glamour, what wild will,
Transfigure the shadows? Whose,
Heart of my heart, Soul of my soul, but yours?

Ghosts, ghosts, the sapphirine air
Teems with them even to the gleaming ends
Of the wild day-spring! Ghosts,
Everywhere, everywhere, till I and you
At last dear love, at last!
Are in the dreaming, even as Life and Death,
Twin-ministers of the unoriginal Will.

XI

Gulls in an aery morrice
Gleam and vanish and gleam . . .
The full sea, sleepily basking,
Dreams under skies of dream.

Gulls in an aery morrice
Circle and swoop and close . . .
Fuller and ever fuller
The rose of the morning blows.

Gulls in an aery morrice
Frolicking float and fade . . .
O the way of a bird in the sunshine,
The way of a man with a maid!

XII

Some starlit garden grey with dew,
Some chamber flushed with wine and fire,
What matters where, so I and you
Are worthy our desire?

Behind, a past that scolds and jeers
For ungirt loin and lamp unlit;
In front the unmanageable years,
The trap upon the pit;

Think on the shame of dreams for deeds,
The scandal of unnatural strife,

The slur upon immortal needs,
The treason done to life:

Arise! no more a living lie
And with me quicken and control
A memory that shall magnify
The universal Soul.

XIII
(To James McNeill Whistler)

Under a stagnant sky,
Gloom out of gloom uncoiling into gloom,
The River, jaded and forlorn,
Welters and wanders wearily, wretchedly on;
Yet in and out among the ribs
Of the old skeleton bridge, as in the piles
Of some dead lake-built city, fall of skulls,
Worm-worn, rat-riddled, mouldy with memories,
Lingers to babble, to a broken tune
(Once, O the unvoiced music of my heart!)
So melancholy a soliloquy
It sounds as it might tell
The secret of the unending grief-in-grain,
The terror of Time and Change and Death,
That wastes this floating, transitory world.

What of the incantation
That forced the huddled shapes on yonder short
To take and wear the night
Like a material majesty?
That touched the shafts of wavering fire
About this miserable welter and wash
(River, O River of Journeys, River of Dreams!)
Into long, shining signals from the panes
Of an enchanted pleasure-house
Where life and life might live life lost in life
For ever and evermore?

O Death! O Change! O Time!
Without you, O the insufferable eyes
Of these poor Might-Have-Beens,
These fatuous, ineffectual Yesterdays!

XIV

Time and the Earth
The old Father and Mother
Their teeming accomplished,

Their purpose fulfilled,
Close with a smile
For a moment of kindness
Ere for the winter
They settle to sleep.

Failing yet gracious,
Slow pacing, soon homing,
A patriarch that strolls
Through the tents of his children,
The Sun, as he journeys
His round on the lower
Ascents of the blue,
Washes the roofs
And the hillsides with clarity;
Charms the dark pools
Till they break into pictures;
Scatters magnificent
Alms to the beggar trees;
Touches the mist-folk
That crowd to his escort
Into translucencies
Radiant and ravishing,
As with the visible
Spirit of Summer
Gloriously vaporised,
Visioned in gold.

Love, though the fallen leaf
Mark, and the fleeting light
And the loud, loitering
Footfall of darkness
Sign, to the heart
Of the passage of destiny,
Here is the ghost
Of a summer that lived for us,
Here is a promise
Of summers to be.

XV

You played and sang a snatch of song,
A song that all-too well we knew;
But whither had flown the ancient wrong;
And was it really I and you?
O since the end of life's to live
And pay in pence the common debt,
What should it cost us to forgive
Whose daily task is to forget?

You babbled in the well-known voice
Not new, not new, the words you said.
You touched me off that famous poise,
That old effect, of neck and head.
Dear, was it really you and I?
In truth the riddle's ill to read,
So many are the deaths we die
Before we can be dead indeed.

XVI

One with the ruined sunset,
The strange forsaken sands,
What is it waits and wanders
And signs with desperate hands?

What is it calls in the twilight
Calls as its chance were vain?
The cry of a gull sent seaward
Or the voice of an ancient pain?

The red ghost of the sunset,
It walks them as its own,
These dreary and desolate reaches . . .
But O that it walked alone!

XVII
CARMEN PATIBULARE
(To H. S.)

Tree, Old Tree of the Triple Crook
And the rope of the Black Election,
'Tis the faith of the Fool that a race you rule
Can never achieve perfection:
And 'It's O for the time of the New Sublime
And the better than human way
When the Wolf (poor beast) shall come to his own
And the Rat shall have his day!'

For Tree, Old Tree of the Triple Beam
And the power of provocation,
You have cockered the Brute with your dreadful fruit
Till your thought is mere stupration:
And 'It's how should we rise to be pure and wise,
And how can we choose but fall,
So long as the Hangman makes us dread
And the Noose floats free for all?'

So Tree, Old Tree of the Triple Coign

And the trick there's no recalling,
They will haggle and hew till they hack you through
And at last they lay you sprawling:
When 'Hey! for the hour of the race in flower
And the long good-bye to sin!'
And 'Ho! for the fires of Hell gone out
For the want of keeping in!'

But Tree, Old Tree of the Triple Bough
And the ghastly Dreams that tend you,
Your growth began with the life of Man
And only his death can end you:
They may tug in line at your hempen twine,
They may flourish with axe and saw,
But your taproot drinks of the Sacred Springs
In the living rock of Law.

And Tree, Old Tree of the Triple Fork,
When the spent sun reels and blunders
Down a welkin lit with the flare of the Pit
As it seethes in spate and thunders,
Stern on the glare of the tortured air
Your lines august shall gloom,
And your master-beam be the last thing whelmed
In the ruining roar of Doom.

XVIII
(To M. E. H.)

When you wake in your crib,
You, an inch of experience
Vaulted about
With the wonder of darkness;
Wailing and striving
To reach from your feebleness
Something you feel
Will be good to and cherish you,
Something you know
And can rest upon blindly:
O then a hand
(Your mother's, your mother's!)
By the fall of its fingers
All knowledge, all power to you,
Out of the dreary,
Discouraging strangenesses
Comes to and masters you,
Takes you, and lovingly
Woos you and soothes you
Back, as you cling to it,
Back to some comforting

Corner of sleep.

So you wake in your bed,
Having lived, having loved:
But the shadows are there,
And the world and its kingdoms
Incredibly faded;
And you grope in the Terror
Above you and under
For the light, for the warmth,
The assurance of life;
But the blasts are ice-born,
And your heart is nigh burst
With the weight of the gloom
And the stress of your strangled
And desperate endeavour:
Sudden a hand
Mother, O Mother!
God at His best to you,
Out of the roaring,
Impossible silences,
Falls on and urges you,
Mightily, tenderly,
Forth, as you clutch at it,
Forth to the infinite
Peace of the Grave.

XIX

O Time and Change, they range and range
From sunshine round to thunder!
They glance and go as the great winds blow,
And the best of our dreams drive under:
For Time and Change estrange, estrange
And, now they have looked and seen us,
O we that were dear we are all-too near
With the thick of the world between us.

O Death and Time, they chime and chime
Like bells at sunset falling!
They end the song, they right the wrong,
They set the old echoes calling:
For Death and Time bring on the prime
Of God's own chosen weather,
And we lie in the peace of the Great Release
As once in the grass together.

XX

The shadow of Dawn;
Stillness and stars and over-mastering dreams
Of Life and Death and Sleep;
Heard over gleaming flats the old unchanging sound
Of the old unchanging Sea.

My soul and yours
O hand in hand let us fare forth, two ghosts,
Into the ghostliness,
The infinite and abounding solitudes,
Beyond, O beyond! beyond . . .

Here in the porch
Upon the multitudinous silences
Of the kingdoms of the grave,
We twain are you and I, two ghosts Omnipotence
Can touch no more, no more!

XXI

When the wind storms by with a shout, and the stern sea-caves
Exult in the tramp and the roar of onsetting waves,
Then, then, it comes home to the heart that the top of life
Is the passion that burns the blood in the act of strife
Till you pity the dead down there in their quiet graves.

But to drowse with the fen behind and the fog before,
When the rain-rot spreads and a tame sea mumbles the shore,
Not to adventure, none to fight, no right and no wrong,
Sons of the Sword heart-sick for a stave of your sire's old song
O you envy the blessed dead that can live no more!

XXII

Trees and the menace of night;
Then a long, lonely, leaden mere
Backed by a desolate fell
As by a spectral battlement; and then,
Low-brooding, interpenetrating all,
A vast, grey, listless, inexpressive sky,
So beggared, so incredibly bereft
Of starlight and the song of racing worlds
It might have bellied down upon the Void
Where as in terror Light was beginning to be.

Hist! In the trees fulfilled of night
(Night and the wretchedness of the sky)
Is it the hurry of the rain?
Or the noise of a drive of the Dead

Streaming before the irresistible Will
Through the strange dusk of this, the Debateable Land
Between their place and ours?

Like the forgetfulness
Of the work-a-day world made visible,
A mist falls from the melancholy sky:
A messenger from some lost and loving soul,
Hopeless, far wandered, dazed
Here in the provinces of life,
A great white moth fades miserably past.

Thro' the trees in the strange dead night,
Under the vast dead sky,
Forgetting and forgot, a drift of Dead
Sets to the mystic mere, the phantom fell,
And the unimagined vastitudes beyond.

XXIII
(To P. A. G.)

Here they trysted, here they strayed,
In the leafage dewy and boon,
Many a man and many a maid,
And the morn was merry June:
'Death is fleet, Life is sweet,'
Sang the blackbird in the may;
And the hour with flying feet
While they dreamed was yesterday.

Many a maid and many a man
Found the leafage close and boon;
Many a destiny began
O the morn was merry June.
Dead and gone, dead and gone,
(Hark the blackbird in the may!),
Life and Death went hurrying on,
Cheek on cheek and where were they?

Dust in dust engendering dust
In the leafage fresh and boon,
Man and maid fulfil their trust
Still the morn turns merry June.
Mother Life, Father Death
(O the blackbird in the may!),
Each the other's breath for breath,
Fleet the times of the world away.

XXIV

(To A. C.)

What should the Trees,
Midsummer-manifold, each one,
Voluminous, a labyrinth of life
What should such things of bulk and multitude
Yield of their huge, unutterable selves,
To the random importunity of Day,
The blabbing journalist?
Alert to snatch and publish hour by hour
Their greenest hints, their leafiest privacies,
How can he other than endure
The ruminant irony that foists him off
With broad-blown falsehoods, or the obviousness
Of laughter flickering back from shine to shade,
And disappearances of homing birds,
And frolicsome freaks
Of little boughs that frisk with little boughs?

Now, at the word
Of the ancient, sacerdotal Night,
Night of the many secrets, whose effect
Transfiguring, hierophantic, dread
Themselves alone may fully apprehend,
They tremble and are changed:
In each, the uncouth individual soul
Looms forth and glooms
Essential, and, their bodily presences
Touched with inordinate significance,
Wearing the darkness like the livery
Of some mysterious and tremendous guild,
They brood, they menace, they appal:
Or the anguish of prophecy tears them, and they wring
Wild hands of warning in the face
Of some inevitable advance of doom:
Or, each to the other bending, beckoning, signing,
As in some monstrous market-place,
They pass the news, these Gossips of the Prime,
In that old speech their forefathers
Learned on the lawns of Eden, ere they heard
The troubled voice of Eve
Naming the wondering folk of Paradise.

Your sense is sealed, or you should hear them tell
The tale of their dim life and all
Its compost of experience: how the Sun
Spreads them their daily feast,
Sumptuous, of light, firing them as with wine;
Of the old Moon's fitful solicitude
And those mild messages the Stars
Descend in silver silences and dews;

Or what the buxom West,
Wanton with wading in the swirl of the wheat,
Said, and their leafage laughed;
And how the wet-winged Angel of the Rain
Came whispering . . . whispering; and the gifts of the Year
The sting of the stirring sap
Under the wizardry of the young-eyed Spring,
Their summer amplitudes of pomp
And rich autumnal melancholy, and the shrill,
Embittered housewifery
Of the lean Winter: all such things,
And with them all the goodness of the Master
Whose right hand blesses with increase and life,
Whose left hand honours with decay and death.

So, under the constraint of Night,
These gross and simple creatures,
Each in his scores of rings, which rings are years,
A servant of the Will.
And God, the Craftsman, as He walks
The floor of His workshop, hearkens, full of cheer
In thus accomplishing
The aims of His miraculous artistry.

XXV

What have I done for you,
England, my England?
What is there I would not do,
England my own?
With your glorious eyes austere,
As the Lord were walking near,
Whispering terrible things and dear
As the Song on your bugles blown,
England
Round the world on your bugles blown!

Where shall the watchful Sun,
England, my England,
Match the master-work you've done,
England my own?
When shall he rejoice agen
Such a breed of mighty men
As come forward, one to ten,
To the Song on your bugles blown,
England
Down the years on your bugles blown?

Ever the faith endures,
England, my England:

'Take and break us: we are yours,
'England, my own!
'Life is good, and joy runs high
'Between English earth and sky:
'Death is death; but we shall die
'To the Song on your bugles blown,
'England
'To the stars on your bugles blown!'

They call you proud and hard,
England, my England:
You with worlds to watch and ward,
England, my own!
You whose mailed hand keeps the keys
Of such teeming destinies
You could know nor dread nor ease
Were the Song on your bugles blown,
England,
Round the Pit on your bugles blown!

Mother of Ships whose might,
England, my England,
Is the fierce old Sea's delight,
England, my own,
Chosen daughter of the Lord,
Spouse-in-Chief of the ancient Sword,
There's the menace of the Word
In the Song on your bugles blown,
England
Out of heaven on your bugles blown!

www.ingramcontent.com/pod-product-compliance
Lightning Source LLC
Chambersburg PA
CBHW060051050426

42448CB00011B/2406